Helping Children See Jesus

ISBN: 978-1-64104-049-5

The Church
New Testament Volume 15: Acts Part 2

Author: Ruth B. Greiner
Illustrator: Frances H. Hertzler
Colorization Courtesy of Good Life Ministries
Typesetting and Layout: Patricia Pope

© 2018 Bible Visuals International
PO Box 153, Akron, PA 17501-0153
Phone: (717) 859-1131
www.biblevisuals.org

All rights reserved. No part of this publication may be reproduced, stored in a retrieval system or transmitted in any form by any means, electronic, mechanical, photocopy, recording or otherwise, without the prior permission of the publisher, except as provided by USA copyright law.

RELATED ITEMS

To access related items (such as activities, memory verse posters and translated texts) please visit our web store at www.biblevisuals.org and enter 1015 at the top right of the web page. You may need to reduce the zoom setting to get the search box.

FREE TEXT DOWNLOAD

To obtain a FREE printable copy of the English teaching text (PDF format) under Product Format, please scroll down and select Extra–PDF Teacher Text Download. Then under Language select English before clicking the ADD TO CART button to place in your shopping cart. Other languages are available at an additional cost from the Language menu. When checking out, use coupon code XTACSV17 at checkout and click on Apply Coupon to receive the discount on the English text.

Christ is the Head of the Church: and He is the Saviour of the body. Ephesians 5:23b

© Bible Visuals International Inc

Lesson 1
THE CHURCH–PROMISED AND BEGUN

NOTE TO THE TEACHER

If we were to list Bible doctrines in the order of their importance, the list would probably begin this way:

1. Salvation by grace
2. The true Church

It is important, therefore, that your pupils know about the Church.

The Church had its beginning on the Day of Pentecost. It could not have come before that, for Christ had to die in order to redeem the Church. It had to be purchased with His blood. The Church could not have begun before the resurrection of Christ, for He had to be raised from the dead so its members could have resurrection life. The Lord Jesus had to ascend to Heaven before the Church began, so He could be the Head of the Church. The Church could not build itself. It had to wait for the Holy Spirit to come for that very purpose. On the same day that the Holy Spirit came to earth, the Church came into being. To the Christian, therefore, the Day of Pentecost is significant.

Today, in some parts of the world, the word "Church" has come to mean a building in which people meet. But when it began, the word "Church" meant people–called-out ones. Called-out ones are believers who have been called out from among unbelievers.

If your students are true believers in Jesus Christ, they belong to the Church. In these lessons they will learn the answers to some vital questions:

1. How and when did the Church begin?
2. What is the Church like?
3. What does the Church do?
4. What is the message of the Church?

Scripture to be studied: Matthew 16:13-20; Mark 8:27-30; Luke 9:18-20; Ephesians 2:19-22; 1 Peter 2:4-8; Psalm 118:22-23

The *aim* of the lesson: To show how and when the church began.

What your students should *know*: Those who believe in Jesus Christ as Saviour are living stones in Christ's Church.

What your students should *feel*: A desire to be a part of the church.

What your students should *do*:
Unsaved: Believe on the Lord Jesus as Saviour.
Saved: Tell someone this week about the Lord Jesus.

Lesson outline (for the teacher's and students' notebooks):

1. God promised to send His Son to earth (Genesis 3:15).
2. Jesus Christ made many promises (John 14:16).
3. Jesus Christ promised to build His church on Himself (Matthew 16:18).
4. Jesus Christ is the cornerstone of the church (1 Peter 2:6-7).

The verse to be memorized:

Christ is the Head of the Church: and He is the Saviour of the Body. (Ephesians 5:23b)

THE LESSON

Whenever God promises that He will do a certain thing, He does it. Sometimes it takes many, many years–even hundreds of years–for a promise to come true. But in God's time He keeps His promises.

1. GOD PROMISED TO SEND HIS SON TO EARTH
Genesis 3:15

Show Illustration #1

In the long ago, God the Holy Spirit breathed on men of His choosing, causing them to write the Word of God. That Word–the Bible–has been wonderfully kept for us. And in the Bible, God has recorded many promises. One promise that God made was that His Son would come from Heaven to earth. God made that promise as soon as the first man and woman (Adam and Eve) sinned. (See Genesis 3:15.) Sin has always separated man from God. And the only One who could bring man and God together is the Son of God. Because of that, God promised He would send His Son. He repeated that promise again and again, even promising that His Son would be born of a virgin. (See Isaiah 7:14.) He would not have an earthly father. God also promised that His Son would be born in Bethlehem. (See Micah 5:2.)

Year upon year the people of God waited for His Son to come. Sometimes they must have felt as if God had forgotten. For, from the time of His first promise, they had to wait 1,000, 2,000, 3,000, 4,000 years until His Son came to earth. (*Teacher:* Move your finger across the bottom line. Each mark on the line represents 1,000 years.)

2. JESUS CHRIST MADE MANY PROMISES
John 14:16

Show Illustration #2

So that wise men and simple would understand that His Son had come, God announced His coming in two ways: (1) To the wise men who knew the stars, He caused a particular star in the sky to let them know that His Son was on earth. (*Teacher:* Point to the star.) (2) To shepherds, He sent an angel to tell them, "To you . . . is born the Saviour . . . Christ the Lord." (Point to angel and manger.) God had kept His promise.

While God the Son was on earth, He too made certain promises. One promise was that after He died (point to cross), was buried, and rose again (point to empty tomb) and returned to Heaven, the Holy Spirit would come to earth. Once when He spoke of the Spirit of God, the Lord Jesus mentioned the wind. (See John 3:8.) So, when Jesus returned to Heaven (point to arrow) and God sent His Holy Spirit to earth, there was a sound from Heaven like a mighty rushing wind. (See Acts 2:2-3.) And tongues like fire rested upon each one who had been waiting for His coming. (Point to men and tongues of fire.) God the Son had kept His promise. The Holy Spirit had come.

– 18 –

3. JESUS CHRIST PROMISED TO BUILD HIS CHURCH ON HIMSELF
Matthew 16:18

There were other promises which the Son of God made while He was on earth. And it is about one of those promises that we shall be studying in this series. Here is what happened:

One day (before His death) Jesus asked His disciples: "Who do men say that I am?"

The disciples had heard what people were saying about Jesus so they told Him what they had heard: "Some say that You are John the Baptist. Some say that you are Elijah. (Elijah was a prophet who had lived long before.) Someone else says that You must be Jeremiah or one of the other prophets."

Then Jesus asked, "But who do *you* say that I am?"

Simon Peter answered, "You are the Christ, the Son of the living God."

Jesus replied, "No human person has told you this. It has been revealed to you by God the Father in Heaven. You, Peter, are a living stone–a piece of a rock."

Show Illustration #3

Then, doubtless pointing to Himself, Jesus made this glorious promise, "Upon this Rock (I, Myself–the Son of the living God), I will build My church. And the powers of hell shall not overcome it." (See 1 Corinthians 10:4; 1 Peter 2:6-8.)

When did the Lord Jesus keep His promise? When did He start to build His Church? It was on the Day of Pentecost, after He had returned to Heaven. The Holy Spirit came down and immediately lived within the believers, changing them completely.

Peter, for example (before the crucifixion of Christ) had three times denied that He even knew the Lord Jesus. But when the Holy Spirit came and lived in him, Peter the denier became Peter the preacher. What did he preach? He preached that *Jesus is Lord and Christ, the Promised One sent from God.* (Compare Matthew 16:16 with Acts 2:36.) To whom did he preach? He preached to thousands of the very same people who had crucified the Lord Jesus. Why had they crucified Him? Because He had said that He was *Christ, the Son of God.* (See Matthew 26:63-66.) What happened when Peter told them they were guilty and that they should repent of their sin of rejecting Christ? In one day, about 3,000 of them received Christ, believing in Him, the Son of God. Because they were then Christian believers, they at once became part of Christ's Church. Jesus had begun to build His Church, just as He had promised.

Those believers were united to each other. They loved each other. They met together in the temple area and in the homes of one another. They shared what they had with those who were in need. They continually praised God. Each day more people were saved. And the newly saved believers also became part of the Church.

It was on the Day of Pentecost that Jesus began to keep the promise He had made when He told Peter, "I will build My Church." Today, almost 2,000 years later, He is still keeping that promise, for He is still building His Church.

4. JESUS CHRIST IS THE CORNERSTONE OF THE CHURCH
1 Peter 2:6-7

There was more to the promise of Jesus. His promise was: "Upon this Rock (I, Myself–the Son of the living God) I will build My Church." A strong building must have a good foundation. A stone building has a cornerstone–a large stone which is built right into the foundation and unites two walls. And the Lord Jesus promises that He Himself was the Rock, the Foundation-Cornerstone of His Church.

Show Illustration #4

Peter always remembered that promise. Some years later he wrote in one of his letters: "Come to Christ. He is the worthy, living Foundation Rock which God builds upon. By coming to Him, you become living stones in His Building. He is the precious Cornerstone of His Building. (Compare 1 Peter 2:6 with Isaiah 28:16.) Some have rejected Him, but God has made Him the important part of the Building." (Compare 1 Peter 2:7 with Psalm 118:22.)

Who is the Cornerstone of the Church? The Lord Jesus Christ. (*Teacher:* Draw a line from large stone in picture to illustration of Christ.) Who are the living stones in Christ's Church? Those who come to the Lord Jesus and receive Him as Saviour. People like you, like me; people who are different from us. Men, women, children; rich and poor; highlanders and lowlanders; farmers, teachers, doctors. No matter what color their skin, what kind of clothes they wear, or what kind of work they do–all who believe in Christ, the Son of the living God and receive Him as Saviour, are living stones in Christ's Church.

If we were to give names to the stones in our pictures, what would we name them? (*Teacher:* If you want to write on the stones, use a pencil, so the writing may be erased later.) Let us call this one James (or Andrew, Peter, or any of the other apostles). Are the apostles the only ones who belong to the Church? No, if you have believed in the Lord Jesus Christ and received Him as your personal Saviour, you are part of His Church. You, too, are a living stone in His Building. (Use the names of saved students for naming other stones in the picture.)

Why is the building in the picture not complete? Because the Church is still being built. On the Day of Pentecost Peter preached: "Whoever will call on the name of the Lord shall be saved." And 3,000 people were added to the true Church that day. Ever since that time the Church has been growing. Every day "living stones" are being added to the Building. And do you know what will happen when the Church is complete? Jesus Christ will come for His Church. He will take it to be with Him forever.

Until that day we must all help to build the Church. Peter and James and John and the other apostles let God use them to bring new believers–living stones–into the Church.

Are *you* a living stone in Christ's Church? You are if you have really believed in Jesus Christ as your Saviour. If so, do you care about others? Does it matter to you that many are not safely in His Church as you are? Will you help to gather new living stones this week?

Lesson 2
THE CHURCH—WHAT IT DOES

NOTE TO THE TEACHER

In the verse which we are memorizing, the Church is spoken of as *the Body of Christ*). (See Ephesians 1:22-23; Colossians 1:24.) As a physical body must have a head, so the Body of Christ (believers–the Church) must have a Head. And the Head of the Church is Christ. (See Colossians 1:18.)

It is correct, therefore, to speak of Christ's Church as *His Building* or *His Body*. In each instance, we remember that the most important part of the Church is Christ Himself. If we refer to His Church as His Building, we recall that the most important part of a building is the foundation-cornerstone. Or, if we refer to the Church as the Body of Christ, we think of the most important part of the physical body–the head. Just so, Christ has first place in His Church.

There are two expressions in the Book of the Acts which you ought to underline: (1) "With one accord," and (2) "With gladness." The early Church had unity and joy. This must have pleased the Lord Jesus Christ, who, in one of His last prayers on earth prayed, "Holy Father, keep all those You have given Me in your care, so *that they may be united,* as We are . . . That their hearts may be *filled with My joy*" (John 17:11,13).

The unity and joy of the believers must have been observed by the unbelievers in Jerusalem. Do unbelievers around you see you and your fellow believers unified and joyous?

According to Acts 2:41-42, there were five practices of the early Church:

1. The new believers were immediately baptized, to witness to others that they had received Christ as Saviour. (See Acts 10:44-48.)
2. They faithfully listened to the apostles who taught them the Word of God.
3. They met together to study the Word of God. Along with studying the Word, they also shared experiences–and even their money.
4. They broke bread (had Communion–the Lord's Supper) together.
5. They prayed together.

Scripture to be studied: Acts 2:37-47; 4:32-37; 1 Corinthians 12:12-31; Ephesians 1:22-23

The *aim* of the lesson: To show what the church does and the importance of each member.

What your students should *know*: Jesus Christ is the Head–the most important part of the Church.

What your students should *feel*: Thankful to God for making it possible for them to be members of His Church.

What your students should *do*: Allow the Lord Jesus to guide them in their daily decisions.

Lesson outline (for the teacher's and students' notebooks):

1. The Church grows (Acts 2:37-41).
2. The Church learns the Word of God (Acts 2:42-43).
3. The Church fellowships together (Acts 4:32-37).
4. The Church observes the Lord's Supper (Acts 2:46; 1 Corinthians 11:23-26).

The verse to be memorized:

Christ is the Head of the Church: and He is the Saviour of the Body. (Ephesians 5:23b)

REVIEW

1. Who came down from Heaven on the Day of Pentecost? (*The Holy Spirit*)
2. When did the true Church begin? (*On the Day of Pentecost when the Holy Spirit came down to live in believers*)
3. Who is the Foundation-Cornerstone of the true Church? (*The Lord Jesus Christ*)
4. Who are the living stones in Christ's Church? (*Everyone who has believed in Jesus Christ as Saviour*)

THE LESSON

Something wonderful had happened in Jerusalem. People were talking about it in their homes. They talked about it on the streets and in the marketplaces. The Lord Jesus Christ had begun to build His Church. It was not a building made of mud or wood or stones. It was built differently from any building which you or I could imagine.

1. THE CHURCH GROWS

Acts 2:37-41

Show Illustration #4

Jesus Christ, the Son of God, was the Foundation-Cornerstone of the Church. The stones in this Building were people. Peter was one of these stones. So were James and Philip and Bartholomew and Matthias and the other apostles. They had become part of this living Building (the Church) by accepting the Son of God who died for their sins and had risen from the dead.

Could anyone become a part of this Building? Oh yes! When Peter preached to a great crowd on the Day of Pentecost, he said that the good news of salvation was for everyone. Peter did not say, "If you pay enough money to the Church, you may be forgiven and be a part of the Building of Christ." Nor did he say, "If you are a good person, you may come." But he did say, "Whoever will call on the name of the Lord will be saved" (Acts 2:21).

Imagine that! He told the very same people who had been responsible for the crucifixion and death of the Lord Jesus Christ, that they could be saved. (See Acts 2:23.)

Peter also said in his first sermon, "God has raised Jesus up from death. And He has made this same Jesus, whom you have crucified, both Lord and Christ."

Immediately many were pricked in their hearts. "What shall we do?" they cried.

Peter answered, "Repent and be baptized, everyone of you, in the name of Jesus Christ. This is the way you can let people know that you believe that He is the Son of the living God."

Show Illustration #5

At once, 3,000 people turned to Christ Jesus. And that very day they were baptized. (*Teacher:* If any of your pupils question why we have pictured the baptism taking place in the water, show them Mark 1:9-10; Acts 8:36-39; Romans 6:3-5.)

The next day more men and women and children believed. And there were more the day after that. Immediately these new believers became part of the Church. Day after day the Church kept growing.

People in and around Jerusalem who did not believe in Jesus, watched what was happening. They heard people praying to God, asking His forgiveness and confessing that they believed in Jesus Christ, the Son of the living God. The unbelieving crowds watched as the new believers were baptized. They saw the believers going to the temple each day. They heard them praising and worshiping God. They saw the joy that the believers had. They observed that the believers truly loved each other. They saw the believers helping those who were in need. *Why are these people so changed?* the unbelievers wondered.

The answer was simple. The believers were allowing the Holy Spirit who lived within them to control their lives. Through His power they were Christlike. They were filled with love. They had joy instead of sadness; peace instead of fear; goodness in place of evil. The unbelievers were impressed. Did they like what they saw?

2. THE CHURCH LEARNS THE WORD OF GOD
Acts 2:42-43

Just as the Church of Christ was growing in numbers, each member was growing spiritually. That is, each was becoming more like the Lord Jesus. But to become like Him, they had to know more about Him. Until now, they had hated Him!

Show Illustration #6

So the apostles taught them from the Word of God. (Which was at that time written on scrolls. There were no books as we have them today.) The believers listened carefully to the teachings of the apostles. They had much to learn about the new way of life which Jesus had given them.

3. THE CHURCH FELLOWSHIPS TOGETHER
Acts 4:32-37

Show Illustration #7

The believers met together and talked of the wonderful things they were learning. They had love for God and love for one another–a love which they never had before. So great was their new love that they cared more for each other than for the things which they owned. Their love caused Barnabas and others to sell their land so that they could help the poor people among them. Things such as money, land and fine clothing were not important to them. God their Father, His Word, and His will were all-important. These believers belonged to God and to each other. And they were glad to share all that they had.

In yet another practice the new believers were different from the unbelievers: they broke bread together.

4. THE CHURCH OBSERVES THE LORD'S SUPPER
Acts 2:46; 1 Corinthians 11:23-26

Show Illustration #8

That is, before the Lord Jesus returned to Heaven, He had told His disciples to remember His death. (See Matthew 26:26-30; Mark 14:22-25; Luke 22:17-20.) To do this, they were to break bread and remember His broken body. And they were all to drink from the cup of wine, remembering that His blood was given for the forgiveness of the sins of the world. So the thousands of new believers shared bread and wine together, remembering how much their Saviour had suffered for them.

Probably as part of their service of remembering His death, and certainly at other times, the believers prayed together. They, like the Lord Jesus Himself, appreciated the value of prayer to their heavenly Father.

The believers were the most joyful people in all of Jerusalem. Why? For at least five reasons:

1. They were obediently baptized as the Lord Jesus Himself had commanded. (See Matthew 28:18-19). Show Illustration #5.
2. They studied the Word of God with the apostles as their teachers. Show Illustration #6.
3. They studied the Word themselves, and along with studying the Word, they also shared experiences–and even their money. Show Illustration #7.
4. They faithfully remembered their Lord's death by breaking bread together. Show Illustration #8.
5. They prayed together.

Others who observed their unity and joy wanted to be like them. And each day more people believed in the Lord Jesus Christ. So the Church, which He had promised to build, had new living stones.

God speaks of the Church as being a Building, it is true. But He also speaks of it as something else. Our memory verse tells us: "Christ is the Head of the Church; and He is the Saviour of the Body [of Christ]." Here the Church is called "The Body [of Christ]." How is the Church like a body? You have a body. Your body is made up of different parts. You have arms, hands, fingers, legs, feet, toes. So when the Bible says that the Church is the Body of Christ, it means it is like a body with many parts. All believers are part of the Church [the Body of Christ]. Each one is a separate and necessary part of it.

Suppose your foot could talk and would say, "Since I am not the hand, I am not part of the body." That would be foolish. Suppose your ear would say, "Because I am not the eye, I am not part of the body." Or let us imagine that your whole body was an eye. Then how could you hear? Or if your whole body were an ear, how could you see or smell or talk? But God has made every part of your body for its proper use. Some parts are more important than other parts, but each has its place. (See 1 Corinthians 12:12-27.)

Are you glad that your two feet get along well together? What would happen if one foot said to the other foot, "I will not walk with you today." Or suppose one foot decided to go one direction, and the other foot insisted on going the opposite way. What a terrible time you would have!

Just as your feet must get along well together, so the different members of the Body of Christ must get along well together. It should not matter if others have more honored places in the Body of Christ. It should not matter if someone else seems to have more important work to do. We must all work together with love and with joy so that many new members will be added to the Body of Christ–His Church.

Let us never forget the verse we have been memorizing: the Lord Jesus Christ is the Head of the Church. Just as your mind gives directions to the rest of your body, so the Lord Jesus guides His Church. He is the most important part of the Church.

Right now, let us bow in worship and thanksgiving to God for making a way for us to become members of His Body, the Church.

Lesson 3
THE MESSAGE OF THE CHURCH

Scripture to be studied: Acts 2, 4, 8, 10, 11

The *aim* of the lesson: To show what the message of the church is and its importance.

What your students should *know*: Those who do not hear about the Lord Jesus and accept Him are separated from God forever.

What your students should *feel*: Grateful to the Lord for sending someone to tell them about Jesus Christ.

What your students should *do*: Think of some friend who does not know Jesus Christ as Saviour and witness to him this week.

Lesson outline (for the teacher's and students' notebooks):

1. Salvation is the message of the church (Acts 4:10-12).
2. The Church witnesses to unbelievers, telling of Christ's resurrection (Acts 4:1-2; 6:7).
3. There is one choice: to accept or reject Christ (Matthew 7:13-14).
4. Jesus Christ forgives sins (Acts 10:39-43).

The verse to be memorized:

Christ is the Head of the Church: and He is the Saviour of the Body. (Ephesians 5:23b)

NOTE TO THE TEACHER

You have taught from this volume, (1) *The Beginning of the Church* and (2) *What the Church Does*. Now you are about to teach (3) *The Message of the Church*.

The message of the Church is very important: Salvation (by grace) through faith in the Lord Jesus Christ. (See Acts 15:11.)

THE LESSON

Before the Lord Jesus returned to Heaven, He promised His apostles that they would be His witnesses. As His witnesses, Jesus said they were to go to Jerusalem–the very place where He had been crucified. He told them, further, that they were to go to all of Judea. (Jerusalem was the capital of the province of Judea.) They were also to tell of Him, He said, in Samaria. At that time the Jews had nothing to do with the Samaritans. When they traveled between Galilee and Judea, they would go all the way over to the east coast of the Jordan River rather than go through Samaria. (*Teacher:* Indicate these places on the back page map.) But the Lord Jesus had said that they would tell of Him in Samaria. Imagine that! And, He said, they would go to the ends of the earth, telling of Him. (See Acts 1:8.)

When Jesus went up to Heaven, the Holy Spirit came down and lived in believers. From then on the believers were known as "the Church"–the *called-out ones*. They were called out from among the unbelievers. Because God the Holy Spirit was living in them, they had power to be His witnesses. And He led them. (See Romans 8:14.) to the very places that the Lord Jesus had said they would go. How long did the Church wait before beginning to obey His command? What did they say when they witnessed? What were the results of their witness? We shall see in our lesson today.

Immediately after the Spirit of God came down, Peter fearlessly witnessed to the people gathered in Jerusalem–the very people who had demanded the death of the Lord Jesus. Peter told them, "Whoever will call on the name of the Lord shall be saved . . . We all are witnesses that God raised Jesus from the dead . . . You people have crucified Jesus. But God has made Him Lord–the One to be worshipped. He is the One sent from God." (See Acts 2:21, 32, 36.) About 3,000 of those who heard Peter speak believed on the Lord Jesus as the Son of God and, after receiving Him as Saviour, were baptized.

Shortly after that Peter spoke to some of the religious leaders, including two who had conducted the trials of Jesus (Annas and Caiaphas). He told them, "You crucified Jesus Christ. But God raised Him from the dead. You tried to do away with Him, as builders get rid of an unwanted stone. God has made Him the important Foundation-Cornerstone of His Building." (Peter remembered that Jesus had promised to build His Church upon Himself.) To those who had judged Jesus guilty of death, Peter added, "There is salvation in no one else. There is no one else under Heaven–no one but the Lord Jesus Christ–who can save you."

1. SALVATION IS THE MESSAGE OF THE CHURCH

Acts 4:10-12

Show Illustration #9

What did Peter mean when he spoke of *salvation* and of One who could *save*? He knew the teachings of Jesus: that everyone is on a broad way–a way which leads to destruction in the lake of fire. (See Matthew 7:13-14.) That place was prepared for the devil and his angels. (See Matthew 25:41.) God does not want anyone else to go there. And no one need go to that awful place. God has done everything He could do to keep people from the fire of hell. He wants everyone to be forever with Him in His beautiful Heaven-home.

By giving the Lord Jesus Christ to die on the cross, God put up a blockade on the broad road which leads to destruction. Those who would believe in Him, the Saviour, would be safe. Then, instead of continuing on the broad road, the very moment they believe in Him, they enter the narrow way that leads to life everlasting in Heaven.

Think of it! Even those evil men who had crucified the Lord Jesus were offered God's gift of salvation. Did they receive it? They did not! Instead, they commanded Peter and all the Church not to teach about Jesus or even to speak of Him. (See

Acts 4:18-31.) So, by refusing Him who died on the cross for them, they continued on the broad road that leads to the lake of fire, hell.

2. THE CHURCH WITNESSES TO UNBELIEVERS, TELLING OF CHRIST'S RESURRECTION
Acts 4:1-2; 6:7

Show Illustration #10

In addition to speaking of the death of Christ, the apostles spoke also of His resurrection. Other teachers had lived and died–and stayed dead. The Lord Jesus Christ alone rose from the dead. This truth the first Church emphasized over and over again. (See for example, Acts 2:32; 4:2, 10, 33; 5:30; 10:40; 17:3.) The message of salvation is the message of a risen, living Christ. (See 1 Corinthians 15:3-4.)

The Lord Jesus had foretold that the Church would witness of Him in the very city where He had been crucified. And they did. What were the results of their witness? Multitudes of men and women believed in the Lord Jesus. (See Acts 4:4; 5:14; 6:7.) Did the religious leaders believe? No, they did not! The Church obeyed the command of the Lord to witness. But the men who had hated the Lord Jesus while He was on earth, hated His witnesses also. So they punished them and put them in jail. Did this stop the Church from witnessing? I should say not! God miraculously released the prisoners, and they went to the temple and to every house telling people that they could be saved by believing in the Lord Jesus Christ and receiving Him.

By the time a year had passed, the Church had obeyed the command of Jesus to go to Judea. (*Teacher:* Using the map on the outside back cover, show all the places mentioned as you speak of them.) Philip went way down to the desert. On the road toward Gaza he saw an important man of Ethiopia riding in a chariot. That man had been up in Jerusalem worshipping God. Now, on his way home, he was reading part of the Word of God–something which Isaiah the prophet had written 700 years before. The Holy Spirit told Philip that he should go talk to the man, and Philip ran to obey. "Do you understand what you are reading?" he asked. The Ethiopian replied, "How can I, unless some man teaches me?" And he begged Philip to get up into the chariot with him.

Philip, using the verses which the man had been reading (Isaiah 53:7-8), and others, told him about Jesus. Immediately that man believed in Jesus. Then seeing some water, the Ethiopian exclaimed, "Look at the water! May I be baptized?" And Philip baptized him. As soon as they came up out of the water, the Spirit of God took Philip to Azotus and he preached the good news there and in every city along the way to Caesarea.

In Joppa, it was Peter who preached. And there "many believed in the Lord" (Acts 9:38-42). When he preached in Lydda and Sharon, all who lived there turned to the Lord (Acts 9:35).

The early Church obeyed Jesus Christ and witnessed of His death and of His resurrection. They explained the necessity of believing that Jesus is God the Son and that He must be received as Saviour.

3. THERE IS ONE CHOICE: TO ACCEPT OR REJECT CHRIST
Matthew 7:13-14

Show Illustration #11A

As a result of their witness, people had to make a decision. They knew that the Lord Jesus Christ had died. They understood that He rose from the dead. They had to choose between believing in Him and going His way, or not believing in Him and going their own way.

Show Illustration #11B

Many chose to continue on the broad way that leads to destruction–everlasting separation from God. The fact that the Lord Jesus had died on the cross for them meant nothing to them. It was as if they trampled His precious blood under their feet. (See Hebrews 10:29.)

Show Illustration #11C

But others who heard of the Lord Jesus, turned from the broad road onto the narrow road that leads to life everlasting. They truly believed that Jesus is the Son of the living God and received Him as Saviour. How did they let others know that they had believed in Jesus? They were baptized. (See Matthew 28:19; Acts 2:41; 8:38.)

The Church obeyed the Lord by witnessing of Him in Jerusalem and Judea. Where else had he said they were to go? To Samaria–where no Jew would go. (Show Samaria on the map, please.) Did they obey Him? Yes, Philip preached about Christ in the city of Samaria. (See Acts 8:5.) Peter preached in Caesarea. What do you suppose he preached there? The same thing: the Lord Jesus died on the cross and God raised Him up the third day. And he added that whoever believes in Him shall receive forgiveness of sins. (See Acts 10:39-43.)

4. JESUS CHRIST FORGIVES SINS
Acts 10:39-43

What did it mean to have "forgiveness of sins"?

Show Illustration #12

Every unbeliever felt as if he had a great load on him. It was the load of sin. Each one knew himself to be a sinner– he had lied, cheated, been unkind. His sins weighed him down. He could not get free from them. But the moment he recognized Jesus Christ as the Son of God and believed that He took upon Himself the punishment for the sins of the world–that very moment the load was gone. His sins were forgiven! This was the message that the Church preached.

The Lord Jesus had commanded the Church to tell of Him in Jerusalem, Judea, Samaria, and to the ends of the earth. And within only eight or nine years they had gone up to Phoenecia, Cyprus Island, and to Antioch in Syria. (See Acts 11:19.) Always they preached about the Lord Jesus Christ: His death, His resurrection, His willingness to forgive sin. Their witness had power because the Holy Spirit controlled them. So great numbers believed and turned to the Lord. (See Acts 11:21, 24.)

Those who believed, immediately became witnesses also. The man from Ethiopia went home rejoicing. Surely he told the people in his land of Africa about the One in whom he had believed. So the Word of God spread to the world.

What was begun so long ago continues today. Someone told me that the Lord Jesus is the Son of God, that He loved me and proved it by dying for me. They told me He did not stay dead, but that He arose and He lives. I believed the message. I received the Lord Jesus as my Saviour and He forgave my sins. To prove that I believed Him–and to obey Him–I was baptized. (*Teacher:* Do not say this unless you have believed in Him and have been baptized.) I have been telling the same message to you. If you have believed in the Lord Jesus and received Him as your Saviour, then it is your responsibility–as a member of His Body, the Church–to tell the same message to others. And others will tell it to yet others.

Suppose someone had not given the message to you. You would die and be forever separated from God. Suppose you do not tell the message to others. They may continue on the broad road that leads to the lake of fire, never knowing that Christ died for them. Right this minute think of someone whom you know who has not received the Lord Jesus as Saviour. Mention that name to God in prayer and ask God to help *you* to be the one to witness to that person–this week, if at all possible.

Lesson 4
THE CHURCH

NOTE TO THE TEACHER

As Christians we are witnesses of Jesus Christ. Think of it: God is using you to fulfill His purpose–to complete His Body, the Church, what kind of a witness are you?

As in each of the lessons in this series, there is a lot of teaching material here. If there is more than your students can grasp, divide the lesson and take two class sessions for it.

Take time to explain the illustrations, carefully asking questions to be certain the pupils understand. And, by all means, have them use notebooks. They should either list the main points or draw the illustrations. This way they will be able to review the lessons by themselves. And their notebooks will become their textbook when they teach this information to others.

The *aim* of the lesson: To give an overall view of the Church: its members, its practices, its future.

What your students should *know*: As Christians, Jesus uses them to help build His Church.

What your students should *feel*: A desire to serve Jesus.

What your students should *do*: Witness to someone this week about the Lord Jesus.

Lesson outline (for the teacher's and students' notebooks):

1. God sees everyone as Jews, Gentiles or the Church (1 Corinthians 10:32).
2. Believers practice baptism and the Lord's Supper (Acts 8:38-39; 1 Corinthians 11:23-26).
3. The Church is to witness to the world (Acts 1:8).
4. The Church will reign with Christ (Revelation 19:7-8).

The verse to be memorized:

Christ is the Head of the Church: and He is the Saviour of the Body. (Ephesians 5:23b)

In the Bible God sometimes speaks of His Church (the company of believers) as a Building. (See 1 Corinthians 3:9-11.) At other times He refers to the Church as a Temple (Ephesians 2:20-22). Sometimes He calls the Church His House. (See 1 Timothy 3:15; 1 Peter 2:4-8.) What is the most important part of a beautiful building, a magnificent temple, or a simple house? The foundation.

Show Illustration #4

Who is the Foundation-Cornerstone of the Church? (*The Lord Jesus Christ, the One who holds the whole Building (all believers) together.*)

Who were some of the first living stones in the Church? (*James, Peter, John.*)

When did the Church begin? (*At Pentecost*)

Is the Church now complete? (*No, it is still being built.*)

Who are some living stones recently added to the Building? (*Let the class name those of their number who are new believers.*)

The Bible speaks of the Church by something other than a Building. What is another name for the Church? (*The Body of Christ*)

How is the Church like a Body? (*It has many parts.*)

THE LESSON

Besides being called a Building and a Body, the Church is known as something else. But I am not going to tell you the other name until near the end of the lesson. So you must listen carefully!

1. GOD SEES EVERYONE AS JEWS, GENTILES OR THE CHURCH
1 Corinthians 10:32

Show Illustration #13

You and I usually think of people in one of two ways: either by the color of their skin or by their nationality. We refer to people as having yellow skin, black, brown, red, or white skin. Or we speak of them as Chinese, Africans, Indians, Arabs, or Europeans. (*Teacher:* Name nationalities which your people know.)

But God does not name people by color or by nationality. He divides everyone in all the world into only three groups.

Here on the dark side of the page are stars and stick men. They represent unbelievers who are still in the darkness of sin. On the light side of the page there are also stars and stick men. But they represent believers who have come out of the darkness of sin into God's glorious light.

What is it that separates the believers from the unbelievers? Look closely. It is the cross of the Lord Jesus Christ. The stars and stick men on the right stand for all who have received Christ Jesus as Lord and Saviour. They are no longer controlled by Satan. They have left the broad road that leads to everlasting separation from God. They are on the narrow way that leads to life everlasting in Heaven, God's home.

But why do we have stars at the top of the page on one side and stick men at the bottom? Why are the stars and stick men together on the other side? Let me tell you.

Instead of naming people by color or by nationality God divides everyone in all the world into only three groups: Jews, Gentiles, Church of God. (See 1 Corinthians 10:32.) The Jewish people were chosen by God thousands of years ago for special privileges and responsibilities. (See Romans 9:4-5.) And God said that, like the stars, it would be impossible to count the number of Jews. (See Genesis 15:5.) So we shall call the stars in the illustration, *Jews*. When the Lord Jesus came to earth, He offered Himself and His salvation to the Jews. But they would not receive Him. (See John 1:11-12.) After Pentecost, the first people that the apostles preached to were the Jews. (*Teacher:* If you wish, you may print the word *Jews* at the top left of the page.)

Anyone who is not a Jew is a Gentile. South American, Asian, Indonesian, anyone and everyone who is not a Jew is a Gentile. (*Teacher:* Depending upon the age and understanding of your group, you may want to mention that there are Asian Jews, Mexican Jews, etc.) These stick men represent Gentiles. (*Teacher:* Print *Gentiles* at the bottom left.)

At first the apostles thought that Jews only could be saved. But God showed them that Gentiles could also be saved. And so they preached to the Gentiles. (See Romans 3:9-12; 1 Corinthians 12:13.)

The moment that either Jews or Gentiles are saved, they are members of the Body of Christ. And they are known as *The Church of God*. We may still think of them as either Jewish believers or Gentile believers. But not so with God. Un-believers are either *Jews* or *Gentiles*. Believers (both Jews and Gentiles) are *the Church of God*. Both are saved only one way: by the precious blood of the Lord Jesus Christ. All who come to Him are under His dominion and authority. (*Teacher:* Print *Church of God* on the top right of the page.)

Ever since the Church began at Pentecost (2,000 years ago), it has been growing continually. Each new believer is another stone in the Building; a part of the Body of Christ. In obedience to the Lord Himself, the Church has practiced two ceremonies.

2. BELIEVERS PRACTICE BAPTISM AND THE LORD'S SUPPER

Acts 8:38-39; 1 Corinthians 11:23-26

Show Illustration #14A

The first ceremony helps others to know that we are now believers. How do unbelievers know that we have believed that Jesus is the Son of the living God and that we have received Him as Saviour? By our being baptized. The Ethiopian eunuch, you will remember, was baptized immediately after he had believed in Jesus (Acts 8:38-39).

Show Illustration #14B

The second ceremony helps us to remember the Lord Jesus Christ and the great price He paid to make our salvation possible. This ceremony is known as the *Lord's Supper* or *Communion* or *Breaking Bread*. Just before His death, the Lord Jesus took bread and thanked God for it. Then He broke it and gave it to His disciples to eat. He explained that it represented His body which would soon be broken in death. He then gave them wine as a picture of His blood which He would give for the forgiveness of sin. They were all to drink of it. (Compare Matthew 26:26-29 with 1 Corinthians 11:23-26.) Like the disciples did so long ago, we, the Church, are to do this until He comes to take us to be with Himself.

3. THE CHURCH IS TO WITNESS TO THE WORLD

Acts 1:8

Just before the Lord Jesus returned to Heaven, He promised the disciples that One would come who would give them His power. (See Acts 1:8.) Who is that? (The Holy Spirit.) Did He come? (Yes, He surely did.) Did He live within them and give them power? (Yes, indeed!) For what purpose did they use His power? (To be His witnesses.)

Show Illustration #15

Did the apostles witness? Oh, yes! Where? In Jerusalem, all Judea, even in Samaria, and to the world beyond.

Have you ever thrown a stone into a calm pool of water and noticed how the circles on the surface of the water grew and grew? That is a picture of what happened on the Day of Pentecost when the Church began. Jerusalem was the center point of that great beginning, and from there the Church has spread out farther and farther until now the message has reached you. If you are a part of the Church by faith in the Lord Jesus Christ, the Holy Spirit is living within you. And He is there to give you power to witness to others. If you and I and every believer would be faithful in witnessing, it would not take long for everyone in the whole world to hear the good news of salvation.

Will everyone accept our witness? No, not everyone. Many will reject the gospel. There will be others who will pretend to believe but they will not be true believers in Jesus. But there are those who will listen and believe the Word and open their hearts, truly receiving God's salvation. They will become living stones in the Church. And they will be new witnesses for Jesus Christ.

We have learned how and where the Church began. We have studied that believers are baptized to testify of their salvation. They study the Word of God as it is taught to them. They study the Word with one another and by themselves. Believers are faithful in prayer. They remember the death of the Lord Jesus by taking Communion. The Church is to be known for its unity and its love for others. And the Church is to witness to the world. All of this we know. But what about the future of the Church? Will it continue on and on here on earth? No, it will not. Something wonderful is going to happen to the Church someday–a day which may not be far away. And you will remember the future of the Church if you remember another name for the Church.

4. THE CHURCH WILL REIGN WITH CHRIST
Revelation 19:7-8

You know that the Church is called a Building–all believers are living stones built together with the Lord Jesus, the Foundation-Cornerstone. And you know that the Church is called a Body–all believers are parts of the Body and the Lord Jesus Christ is the Head of the Body. But God gives another name to the Church. It is this: *The Bride of Christ*. (See Ephesians 5:25-27, 31-33; 2 Corinthians 11:2; Revelation 19:7; 21:9.)

When a man and a woman love each other dearly, they want to be together. Sometimes there must be long delays before they can be united. But, because they are promised to each other, they are happy. Finally the day comes. And the one who has prepared a home for his bride comes to get her and takes her to be with himself forever. That is a happy, happy day!

So the Lord Jesus, the One who loves us so much that He gave Himself to die for us, is in Heaven right now preparing a home for His Bride. (See John 14:1-3.) When all who *will* believe in Him, *have* believed, the Bride of Christ will be complete. Then Christ will take His Bride (the believing Church) to be forever with Himself. (See 1 Thessalonians 4:16-17.)

Show Illustration #16

That will be a glorious day for Him–for all whom He bought with His own precious blood will be with Him. And He and His Bride–the Church–will reign together. But if it is a glorious day for Him–that day when He has all believers at His side–think what a day it will be for us! We will remember throughout eternity that He is the One who made it all possible.

There will be some Christians, however, who will be ashamed when they see the Lord Jesus–ashamed, because they have not been faithful witnesses of Him. I hope you will not be one of them.

Rather, I hope you will be able to hear Him say to you, "Well done, My good and faithful servant!"

www.ingramcontent.com/pod-product-compliance
Lightning Source LLC
Chambersburg PA
CBHW060805090426
42736CB00002B/165